Animal Life Cycles

Elephant

by Wendy Perkins

amicus readers 2

amicus
readers

Say hello to amicus readers.

You'll find our helpful dog, Amicus, chasing a ball—to let you know the reading level of a book.

A

Learn to Read
Frequent repetition of sentence structures, high frequency words, and familiar topics provide ample support for brand new readers. Approximately 100 words.

1

Read Independently
Repetition is mixed with varied sentence structures and 6 to 8 content words per book are introduced with photo label and picture glossary supports. Approximately 150 words.

2

Read to Know More
These books feature a higher text load with additional nonfiction features such as more photos, time lines, and text divided into sections. Approximately 250 words.

Amicus Readers are published by **Amicus**
P.O. Box 1329, Mankato, Minnesota 56002

U.S. publication copyright © 2012 Amicus.
International copyright reserved in all countries.
No part of this book may be reproduced in any
form without written permission from the publisher.

Series Editor   Rebecca Glaser
Series Designer   Heather Dreisbach
Photo Researcher   Heather Dreisbach

Printed in the United States of America at
Corporate Graphics, in North Mankato, Minnesota.

1023
3-2011

10 9 8 7 6 5 4 3 2 1

Library of Congress Cataloging-in-Publication Data
Perkins, Wendy, 1957-
  Elephant / by Wendy Perkins.
     p. cm. – (Amicus Readers. Animal life cycles)
  Includes index.
  Summary: "Presents the life cycle of an elephant
  from mating and birth to adult. Includes time line
  of life cycle and sequencing activity"–Provided by
  publisher.
  ISBN 978-1-60753-155-5 (library binding)
  1. Elephants–Life cycles–Juvenile literature. I. Title.
QL737.P98P44 2011
599.67–dc22
                                        2010035670

Table of Contents

A Life Cycle

Elephants have a long **life cycle**. They can live to be more than 60 years old. It takes many years for a baby elephant to become an adult.

adolescent

calf

adult

Calf

A baby elephant is called a **calf**. It grows inside its mother's body for 22 months.

calf

Grows inside
mother
22 months

A newborn calf cannot take care of itself.
When the calf drinks its mother's milk, it is
nursing. It begins eating plants, too, when
it is four months old.

Grows inside
mother
22 months

Calf begins
eating plants
4 months old

The calf starts to grow **tusks** between the ages of six months to one year. The calf can't use its small tusks to defend itself. Other elephants in the **herd** protect it from lions and other danger.

Grows inside
mother
22 months

Calf begins
eating plants
4 months old

Tusks start
to grow
6 months –
1 year old

tusk

herd

Adolescent

After the calf stops nursing, it is no longer a baby. It is an **adolescent**. This happens when it is 3 to 5 years old. Its tusks are longer, and they will keep growing.

Grows inside mother
22 months

Calf begins eating plants
4 months old

Tusks start to grow
6 months – 1 year old

Adolescent
3–5 years old

When male elephants are 10 years old, they leave the herd. They often find other young males to live with. Females stay in the herd and learn how to be mothers.

Grows inside mother 22 months	Calf begins eating plants 4 months old	Tusks start to grow 6 months – 1 year old	Adolescent 3–5 years old

Males leave
herd
10 years old

Adult

Elephants become adults when they are about 15 years old. Adult females are called **cows**. Adult males are called **bulls**. Bulls are much bigger than cows.

COW

| Grows inside mother 22 months | Calf begins eating plants 4 months old | Tusks start to grow 6 months – 1 year old | Adolescent 3–5 years old |

Bull elephants live by themselves most of the time. They visit herds of cows for mating. After 22 months, new calves are born.

| Grows inside mother 22 months | Calf begins eating plants 4 months old | Tusks start to grow 6 months – 1 year old | Adolescent 3–5 years old |

Males leave
herd
10 years old

Adult
15 years old

New elephant
calves born
22 months after
mating

Photo Glossary

adolescent

the stage of life
between baby
and adult, like a
human teenager

bull

an adult male
elephant

calf

a baby elephant

cow

an adult female
elephant

herd
a group of elephants that live together

life cycle
the different stages of life from birth to having babies

nursing
how a baby mammal drinks milk from its mother's body

tusk
long, sharp teeth that stick out of an animal's mouth

Life Cycle Puzzle

The stages of an elephant's life are all mixed up.
Can you put them in the right order?

calf nursing

adult

eating plants

adolescent

calf born

tusks grow

Ideas for Parents and Teachers

amicus readers

Children are fascinated by animals, and even more so by life cycles as they grow up themselves. *Animal Life Cycles*, an Amicus Readers Level 2 series, lets kids compare life stages of animals. The books offer support by using labels and a photo glossary to introduce new vocabulary. The activity page and time lines reinforce sequencing skills.

Before Reading
- Read the title and ask the children to tell what they know about babies or baby animals.
- Have the students talk about whether they've seen elephants before.
- Look at the photo glossary words. Tell children to watch for them as they read the book.

Read the Book
- "Walk" through the book and look at the photos. Point out the time line showing how long elephants spend at each stage.
- Ask the students to read the book independently.
- Provide support where necessary. Show students how to use the photo glossary if they need help with words.

After Reading
- Have students do the activity on page 22 and put the stages of the elephant life cycle in order.
- Compare the life cycle of a elephant with other animals in the series. Does it have the same number of stages?
- Have the students compare the human life cycle to an elephant's life cycle. How is it different? How is it the same?

Index

Web Sites

African Elephant: Photos, Video, Facts, E-card, Map—National Geographic Kids
http://kids.nationalgeographic.com/kids/animals/creaturefeature/african-elephant

African Elephant Printout—EnchantedLearning.com
http://www.enchantedlearning.com/subjects/mammals/elephant/Africancoloring.shtml

San Diego Zoo's Animal Bytes: Elephant
http://www.sandiegozoo.org/animalbytes/t-elephant.html

Photo Credits
t=top; b=bottom; l=left; r=right; m=middle
Anup Shah/Getty Images, cover; Ben Cranke/Getty Images, 9, 16, 17, 20tm, 20b, 21bm, 22tl; Four Oaks/Shutterstock, 15; Fuse/Getty Images, 18–19, 21t; James Warwick/Getty Images, 5, 21b, 22tr; Joshua Hodge Photography/iStockphoto, 22ml; Marty Eby/iStockphoto, 21tm; Martyn Colbeck/Photolibrary, 4, 6, 7, 20bm, 22bl; photostaud/Alamy, 4–5, 13, 20t, 22mr; Steve & Ann Toon /Getty Images, 11t, 22br; Villiers Steyn/Shutterstock, 11b; Winfried Wisniewski/Getty Images, 1